STAYING FIT WHILE

YOU SIT

An Active Author Guide for Workplace Wellness

by
CYNTHIA VESPIA

STAYING FIT WHILE YOU SIT

An Active Author Guide for Workplace Wellness

Copyright © 2025 Cynthia Vespia

All rights reserved.

ISBN: 978-1-7376927-7-5

Cover design by Cynthia Vespia via Canva.com

This book is licensed to the original purchaser only. Duplication or distribution via any means is illegal and a violation of International Copyright Law, subject to criminal prosecution and upon conviction, fines and/or imprisonment. No part of this publication may be reproduced, stored in a retrieval system, or transmitted in any form or by any means, electronic, mechanical, photocopying, recording, scanning, or otherwise, without the prior written permission of the author.

Limit of Liability/Disclaimer of Warranty:

This book details the author's personal experiences and opinions about health and wellness. The information provided is for general informational purposes only. All content, including text, graphics, images, and information, is presented as an educational resource and is not intended as a substitute for professional medical advice, diagnosis, or treatment.

The author and publisher are providing this book and its contents on an "as is" basis and make no representations or warranties of any kind with respect to this book or its contents. In addition, the author and publisher do not represent or warrant that the information accessible via this book is accurate, complete, or current.

STAYING FIT WHILE YOU SIT

The author does not recommend or endorse any specific tests, physicians, products, procedures, opinions, or other information that may be mentioned in this book. Reliance on any information provided in this book, its content creators, or others referenced within the book is solely at your own risk.

Neither the author or publisher, nor any authors, contributors, or other representatives will be liable for damages arising out of or in connection with the use of this book.

This is a comprehensive limitation of liability that applies to all damages of any kind, including (without limitation) compensatory; direct, indirect or consequential damages; loss of data, income or profit; loss of or damage to property and claims of third parties.

You understand that this book is not intended as a substitute for consultation with a licensed healthcare practitioner, such as your physician. Before you begin any healthcare program, or change your lifestyle in anyway, you will consult your physician or another licensed healthcare practitioner to ensure that you are in good health and that the examples contained in this book will not harm you.

This book provides content related to physical and/or mental health issues. As such, use of this book implies your acceptance of this disclaimer.

STAYING FIT WHILE YOU SIT

CHAPTERS

Introduction

1. Is sitting the new smoking?
2. The effects of a sedentary life
3. Prevention intervention
    - A blueprint for setting up your workspace
    - Ergonomics and thrones: choosing a chair
    - Using an exercise ball instead of an office chair
    - What's the deal with standing desks?
    - Avoiding carpal tunnel syndrome
    - Why you need to keep your psoas happy
    - A word on foam rollers
4. How exercise impacts the body
    - Benefits of exercise
    - Categories of exercise
    - Aerobic exercise
    - Anaerobic training
    - Flexibility training
5. The Workouts
    - Throwing your bodyweight around

STAYING FIT WHILE YOU SIT

- Can't resist the resistance bands
- Dumbbells by the desk
- How to get in your cardio
- Open the mind and body with yoga
- Making mobility matter

6. Knowing Your Nutrition
   - Avoiding caffeine crash
   - Pack your snacks
   - Why water is so important
   - Make time for lunch
   - What's the deal with meal prepping?
   - How to avoid nutritional sabotage

7. Healthy Life Hacks
   - Where you park matters
   - Pretend the elevator is broken
   - Why you should have face-to-face meetings
   - Act out your action scenes
   - Develop healthy habits for the long term

Sneak Peek – Writing Warrior: An Active Author Guide to Overcoming Adversity and Achieving Goals

Acknowledgments

About the Author

Active Author Guidebook Series

Other Books

INTRODUCTION

If you're like most authors, you've struggled with aches and pains, unbalanced nutrition, eye strain, and more. The longer we sit working on our craft, the more these problems crop up. Writing and other creative professions where you're stuck in a chair can take a mental and physical toll.

I've been where you are, with pain plaguing my hips and hands. My neck and back were worn out, making it unbearable to keep sitting, even though I had work to complete. Sometimes, the pain grew so debilitating that I needed to lie down on a heating pad, completely forfeiting the day.

That type of constant discomfort can keep you from completing your work, enjoying your day, and getting other tasks done. The more you disregard the discomfort, the worse it can get, leading to ongoing pain and health problems.

Fortunately, my background in the fitness industry gave me the tools I needed to maintain my health and wellness throughout my writing career. Now, I want to share those tools with you!

The goal is to launch a counterattack against the strain of sitting. Before the damage becomes too severe, we need to put together a plan focused on whole-body health. Subtle shifts in your work setting, physicality, and nutrition can offset the negative impacts of a sedentary career.

I'm not a physician, so I encourage you to seek out the advice of a medical professional before delving into what I'm offering in the pages of this book.

But I am a former competitive athlete, certified fitness instructor, fantasy author, and wellness writer. I have over 12 years of experience as a coach in physical training and motivation, and double that as an author.

I've seen time and again how a sedentary life can wreak havoc on the body. As I said, I've been there myself. I've been where you are, and I found my way to the other side. Now, I want to show you how to do the same.

It's been my mission to combine my love of writing and wellness to offer practical guides for whole-body health with a specific focus on the writing industry. I want to help my fellow authors break free from limiting patterns to become the healthiest, most creatively productive version of themselves.

During my career as a competitive athlete, I maintained a very strict level of fitness and nutrition. That's NOT what I'm going to ask of you. It's unrealistic to try and maintain a lifestyle that strict at all times. Instead, I'll help you implement small, daily changes that will develop into habits. You'll become a healthier version of yourself without feeling deprived or exhausted. That would be counterproductive! We want you feeling your best so you can be creative and productive.

Within these pages are simple ways for you to incorporate more activity during your day. I'll explain how you can maintain a healthier diet even when you feel slammed with work. You'll learn the best ways to design your workspace. I'll also discuss some healthy life hacks you probably don't know about that will streamline your work/life balance.

All this and more will help you stay fit while you sit!

This is not simply about aesthetics. Our focus will be on reducing pain, increasing energy, and developing healthy habits you can sustain for a lifetime.

Since I am one myself, these guides are aimed at the author community. But honestly, whether you work at an office, work from home, are a gamer, or a graphic designer, these tips can help you find that healthier version of yourself you've been looking for. Share this guide with your friends and loved ones to help them get back on track toward the pursuit of their passions.

Because feeling your best fuels creativity!

Together, we can get you back into a healthy routine and keep you stay there no matter how long you've been off track!

As a rule of thumb and general disclaimer, you should always consult your physician before beginning a new program. The information in this guide is not intended to diagnose any medical condition or to replace your healthcare professional. Rather, it is intended to offer information to help the reader cooperate with physicians and health professionals in a mutual quest for optimum well-being. Consult with your physician before instituting any workout or nutrition changes.

But if you're willing to put in the work and make a few small changes to your daily routine, you'll reap the rewards of a healthier body and a clearer mind. Having those pieces in place will help your creativity flourish.

Authors, it's time to get off your ass!

1. Is Sitting the New Smoking?

Could your job be killing you? That's a rhetorical question, but various studies have been done on the harmful effects of sitting for extended periods, and the results aren't promising.

Some researchers have even said that sitting is now on level or even surpasses smoking as a major detriment to your health. While other studies have refuted those claims, it's still important to point out how the topic became a debate in the first place.

James A. Levine, MD, PhD. was the first to state that "sitting is the new smoking."[1] As director of the Mayo Clinic-Arizona State University Obesity Solutions Initiative, Levine believed that the amount of time many Americans spend sitting each day mirrored the health risks caused by smoking.[2]

Whether sitting is the new smoking or not, it's clear that sitting for over 8 hours every day does put a strain on the body that can develop into more than just discomfort. Additional research has shown there are higher risks of health problems originating from sedentary lifestyles, especially as it relates to older individuals.[3]

Saying that "sitting is the new smoking" is simply a comparison of two silent killers. If these activities are implemented daily without course correction, then each has the capacity to cause irreparable damage. While the addictive and carcinogen effects of smoking outweigh the impact of sitting in terms of disease, this doesn't let sitting off the hook entirely.

Authors are driven by our passion to create. So, when writing our novels, we aren't thinking about what's happening to our posture as we slump over the computer or how the screen time impacts our eyes. If we get into a state of flow, nothing is breaking that.

With the technological advances in the past few decades, most businesses now rely on computers to navigate their company's needs. This means if you have a traditional 9 to 5 job on top of your writing career, you'll be sitting for upwards of ten, twelve, and even fourteen-hour days.

Once the workday ends, you sit in a car to drive home from the office, sit down to dinner, sit in front of the TV to unwind, and then sit at your desk to work on your passion from five to nine. Most of your day is spent on your rear, and it's causing a whole bunch of problems you aren't aware of...yet.

Home-based businesses are also guilty of extensive sitting. If you're lucky enough to be a full-time author, you must still wear multiple hats to navigate your career successfully. This means authors sit for more extended hours even when they aren't engaged in writing the novel.

Aside from the actual writing itself, authors are often on their computers or devices scheduling social media posts, sending out emails, or publishing the book through different channels. Being an author is a full-time job, and much of it entails sitting in front of a screen.

Other self-employed entrepreneurs, such as graphic designers or computer programmers, spend even more time in the seat working extra hours to build their businesses. Maybe you know a book cover artist or a website creator to whom this relates. These entrepreneurs work upwards of eighteen to twenty hours daily to create their dynasty.

It's called "hustle" and "grind," but it's also grinding down your body. There's no denying that the dedication to building a business is admirable, but the risk of the reward still needs to be considered.

All this sitting can increase the risk of developing some severe health conditions down the road. Research has shown how health problems like heart disease, cancer, and diabetes are linked to an increased sedentary lifestyle.[4]

That's because when you sit for long periods, your body no longer works in harmony. As staying seated becomes a routine part of your day, your risk of developing health problems increases.[5]

In the next chapter, I'll detail the exact impact of a sedentary lifestyle on your overall health. Throughout the following chapters, we'll discuss how to combat those issues to stay fit while you sit. I'm going to provide you with ways to improve your health and well-being to continue writing well into your golden years.

These are easy, actionable tips that you can adopt into your busy schedule to maintain a healthier, more productive lifestyle. Because feeling your best fuels creativity!

Let's get started!

2. Effects of a Sedentary Life

You might be tempted to skip this chapter and get to the meat of the matter. But it's important to understand exactly what happens from sitting on your ass all day.

If you don't know the ramifications, then you won't adhere to the changes. Knowledge is a driver that can make you change the habits that are negatively impacting your health. Without knowing, you won't be as motivated to change.

If your regular routine is sitting for hours at a time, whether at a computer, television, or game station, it has a negative effect on both body and mind. The longer the sedentary lifestyle goes on without being corrected, the higher the risk of developing health problems.

These issues can last for many years and include problems in the following areas:

Hips and Back Pain

Sitting in a rigid position with little movement can cause increased muscle tightness. The hip flexors are affected the most as the 90-degree bend in the legs increases strain in this area. Limited mobility can also put pressure on the discs in the lower back. This creates pain and an increased risk of long-term back problems.[6]

Shoulders and Neck

A common aggravation from prolonged sitting is tension in the neck and shoulders. This is often the result of poor posture, where the body slouches and the head drops into the chest. This can lead to a pinched nerve, shoulder impingement, headaches and migraines, or other conditions.[7]

Sluggish Metabolism

Sitting for extended periods on a daily basis can contribute to a slower metabolism. Coupled with a lack of physical activity, a sluggish metabolism can lead to weight gain. As the weight increases, it can put more pressure on the joints, causing increased pain. And when you're in pain you don't want to work out. Sitting for too long is one of the biggest risk factors for developing obesity.[8]

Mental Impact

Besides the physical complications that can arise from a stationary lifestyle, there are other negative attributes. When your body slows down due to a lack of physical activity, it can impact your mental capacity. These cognitive changes can cause "brain fog" or the ability to think clearly.[9] A sedentary lifestyle also increases the risk of stress, depression, and other mood-altering disorders.[8]

STAYING FIT WHILE YOU SIT

If these statistics sound frightening, they should. This is a wake-up call about how serious the negative impact of a sedentary lifestyle can be. But rest assured, there are ways to turn all of it around and reduce your risk of acquiring these health problems or worse.

Adding physical activities into your daily routine, and making small changes to your diet, can put you back on a path toward your healthiest self.

Let's start by designing your desk and workspace to better serve you during your writing. As an author, your desk becomes your second home. That's where you create, where the notes for all your characters live, and the location of your favorite coffee mug.

You've probably designed it to be an inviting space. It welcomes you to do your work without prejudice. You can think there, and just sitting at the desk brings you a sense of joy.

Now, let's set up that space to work for your body as well as your creative mind.

3. Prevention Intervention

Now that we've discussed how sitting for prolonged periods can negatively impact your health, let's talk about mitigating adverse reactions and future problems.

Writing novels means hours in front of a computer typing words into your favorite document. Additional editing and revisions mean more time sitting slumped in front of the screen. Factor in the business part of being a published author and sitting time increases further.

One way to prevent the damage caused by sitting for so many hours is by setting up your workstation effectively. When setting up your desk, computer, and workspace, you'll want to design it with an eye on overall wellness, not just comfort.

Sometimes, what seems comfortable, like slouching or crossing your legs to put the computer on your lap, is not good for you in the long run. Having your workspace work for you makes things more efficient. It helps the body relax so you can more easily tap into your creativity.

Preventative measures like the ones I'm about to lay out can help you remain healthy and comfortable at the same time. By making specific changes to your environment, you can diminish the impact of the issues listed in the last chapter and prevent long-term damage.

These simple hacks may seem small but can make a positive difference in the long run.

Improve Your Posture

How you sit can profoundly impact not only your physical health but also your mentality. The next time you sit down to work, take note of your posture.

You probably begin the day upright with hands on the keyboard, feet flat on the floor, shoulders back, full of energy, and ready to tackle the workload in front of you.

But as the day goes on, you'll notice a change. Your shoulders begin to slump forward, which creates tension in the muscles. Maybe you slide down in your chair, causing an unnatural curve in your back. This puts pressure on your spine.

Then your head dips, or you lean closer to the computer screen to see better, causing eye strain and additional neck tension. This also creates eye strain, which can cause headaches and migraines. Your chest is concave, so your breathing becomes shallow, and fatigue increases.

By the time you get done with your work, you're tired, cranky, and sore. So, you spend the next couple of hours slumped in front of the TV until you crawl off to bed, only to repeat the process the next day.

This creates a pattern of repetition in your body's physiology that exacerbates problems over time. Your body remembers these patterns. And while it will do everything it can to reduce the negative impact of sitting, it starts to break down over time.

Let's end the cycle and fortify the body!

It starts by setting up your workspace in a way that's most effective and beneficial for you. I'm sure you've heard some of this information before as ergonomics becomes more prevalent in daily conversation, but it bears repeating. Believe me when I tell you that implementing some of these small adjustments will make a big difference in how you feel.

A Blueprint to Setting up Your Workspace

Monitor Setup

Authors, writers, and other creatives use computers for the majority of their work. Most office spaces have a computer at each desk, regardless of the work being done. Odds are, no matter your work, you'll be looking at your monitor for most of the day, so getting that setup right will be the centerpiece of your desk blueprint.

Your monitor should be set an arm's length away from you, directly behind the keyboard. This goes for any type of computer. If you prefer to do your writing with a tablet that has a removable keyboard or you have a laptop setup, the monitor should still be at arm's length. If you're using multiple monitors, start with the main screen in the center and set up the others along the sides at an angle that allows you to see without craning your neck.

The important part of this initial setup is to have your monitors at eye level. They shouldn't be too high or too low. You want to have a neutral neck when looking at the screen. Get out of the habit of looking down at a screen, even a phone screen.

Over time, this can create what's known as hyperkyphosis, also called a 'dowager's hump.' This is when the spine's natural backward curve can become overly pronounced, leading to a rounded back and other problems.[10] Keep your head neutral with your shoulders back as often as you can.

Duration of Use

Make no mistake: the health of your eyes and vision is a key component to your overall wellness. We spend so much time looking at the screens of our computers, televisions, phones, and tablets that it is extracting a heavy toll we don't even realize we're paying yet.

Too many hours looking at the iridescent lights of a computer monitor can dry the eyes and begin to hinder productivity. Long periods of monitor use lead to what's called "computer vision syndrome,"[11] which includes dry, irritated eyes, blurred vision, and headaches.

One of the ways to alleviate computer vision syndrome is by adjusting your posture when using digital devices. As I said, keep the screen far enough away so that you're not directly on top of it.

Closing your eyes for a few seconds and resting your palms atop them can also be helpful. Using the '20' rule throughout the day is another good way to help your eyes fully relax.

The steps for the '20' rule are simple:

- Look away from you monitor every 20 minutes.
- Focus on something at least 20 feet away.
- Maintain focus for at least 20 seconds.

Implementing the '20' rule will give your eyes a break from the harsh lights of the screen. You'll be able to focus better and reduce the risk of future problems.

Footrest

The way some chairs are designed, they can drag on your hips if you're not sitting completely upright. You can try to train yourself to maintain perfect posture throughout the day, or you can introduce a little help to offset the inevitable slumping.

Set a footrest approximately 2-5 inches under your desk so you can place your feet flat on it. This elevates your legs so the hips and pelvis don't become overworked trying to keep you upright.

Using a footrest is a simple but effective way to reduce the pressure on your lower back and hips. It also helps maintain alignment throughout the spine.

Ergonomics and Thrones: Choosing a Chair

Chairs have come a long way from the simple design of four legs, a metal backing, and a small seat. Early chair designs were made of wood or hard plastic. They often didn't have cushioning for the seat or chair back.

Now, we have chairs designed for comfort and style. There are even chairs created for specific industries. For example, gaming chairs are made with the needs of a gamer in mind and provide ergonomic comfort for long hours locked in front of a screen. A scooped seat that keeps the gamer closer to the floor. And often a spot on the armrest which houses the controller.

Imagine the chairs they could design for authors: a section to hold previous manuscript drafts, a built-in refrigerator for cold drinks, and speakers to pipe in the soundtrack you need for your story. They might already have those types of chairs, if they don't, they should!

Some people are even eliminating their chairs altogether and introducing standing desks or stability balls. There are advantages and disadvantages to some of these options.

Before choosing to sit on a ball or a personalized throne, let's explore some pros and cons. So many chairs are available to choose from, you might feel like Goldilocks sampling the beds in the 3 Bears house.

Back Support

The first thing to look for when choosing a chair is support for the natural curve of your spine. The backrest should fit comfortably into your lower back. This is especially important if you already experience back issues. Adding an extra cushion can be helpful if you find your back is not fully supported by the chair itself. There are many chairs pre-made with a built-in curvature or padding.

Chair Height

Pay special attention to the height adjustment of the chair. The chair should never be so high that your feet don't reach the floor. You should be able to adjust the height of your chair so that your feet rest flat on the floor or on a footrest, as mentioned. Thighs should be parallel to the floor, and knees should be slightly lower than your hips. Adjusting your office chair to the proper seat height helps minimize stress on the knees and lower back.

Headrest

A headrest provides additional support for your head and takes the pressure off your neck. If you're already dealing with neck issues, a headrest that cradles your head is recommended. Some chairs have cushions supporting the neck, or you can buy an additional removable attachment. The benefit of a removable component is the ability to place it where you'll get the most comfort.

Using an Exercise Ball Instead of a Chair

How can sitting on a ball be comfortable, let alone healthy? Taking an exercise ball out of the gym and into the office is predicated on the idea that the core muscles will be activated more, and this will enable better posture.

To explain further, a stability ball is a large ball filled with air used in fitness programs to increase activation of the trunk muscles or the core. They are meant to improve core strength and balance when used in conjunction with other exercise movements.

The belief is that these benefits will transfer into the office, and the user can increase core strength, improve posture, and decrease discomfort while sitting. Unfortunately, research12 has shown that stability balls cause more problems than solutions when used as a seat and not an exercise tool.

One study found that spinal shrinkage increased with the use of an exercise ball compared to an office chair. They concurred that an ergonomic office chair is better suited than a stability ball.

With most office hours exceeding 8 to 10 hours, it becomes an overwhelming challenge to keep your core muscles engaged. This causes the average person to reposition their feet to stabilize the ball under them.13 This defeats the purpose of using the ball as a chair and actually causes more problems.

Bottom line:

Stability balls are a great tool when used in the manner in which they were designed. But having the ball replace your chair isn't the best answer to improve posture.

I offer you a compromise: Have the ball at your desk and use it for short bouts of exercise, stretching, and, yes, sitting, but keep your traditional desk chair as well.

What's the Deal with Standing Desks?

Because so much attention is now being shown to the negative effects of extensive sitting, some alternative options have been introduced. One of those is the standing desk. The intention of these desks is to allow you to work at your desk while standing rather than staying seated all day.

According to WebMD[14] some of the benefits of a standing desk include:

Increased calorie burn: One study showed that standing at your desk can burn 88 calories an hour. In comparison, sitting burns 80 calories.

Reduced back pain: Sitting long hours tightens your back muscles and causes ongoing pain. Standing desks lessen back pain by improving posture, which is a major contributor to muscle tightness.

Improved work performance: Studies have shown that employees who use standing desks were 45% more productive than those who sat during the day.

However, standing desks have also shown some negative effects as well.

Leg and foot pain: Being on your feet for too long puts more pressure on your knees, hips, and feet. Over time, it leads to pain and stiffness. Shifting your feet or leaning for relief can cause imbalances.

Vein problems: Extensive standing causes the blood to collect in your leg veins. This can lead to varicose veins as the extra blood causes the vein to stretch and grow weaker.

If you're going to use a standing desk, the preferred method is to alternate between sitting and standing. Most of the standing desks allow you the option to move levels so you can gradually work your way into standing more throughout the day.

Before you go shopping, there are a few factors that you should take into consideration.[15] First, determine where your desk will be placed. Measure the depth and width of your space. Like sitting desks, proper ergonomics are important to prevent neck or back strain.

Your arms should be at a 90-degree angle with your wrists in a neutral position. The computer monitor needs to be directly in front of you and at eye level. Your ears, shoulders, and hips should be in a vertical line.

Standing desks aren't ideal for every task: Certain tasks might not be conducive to using a standing desk. As writers and creatives, we often find it easier to do our work when sitting down. So, depending on your writing style, a standing desk may not be the best option.

Avoiding Carpal Tunnel Syndrome

Obviously, an author spends a lot of time typing. We went to great lengths to learn how to type out our manuscripts with speed and efficiency. Even if you're delving into marketing campaigns for your book, your hands will be on the keyboard for extended periods.

This repetitive type of work brings stress injuries along with it. Repetitive stress injuries include damage to muscles, nerves, ligaments, and tendons. It's caused by repeating the same motion repeatedly.

Carpal tunnel syndrome is a common injury caused by repetitive typing movements. This disorder is brought on by swollen, inflammatory ligaments and tendons compressing the median nerve, which passes through a "tunnel" in the wrist and connects the forearm to the hand.

Injury results from repeated use of a muscle group that is harmed more quickly than it can be repaired. This results in a loss of mobility, flexibility, strength, and numbness. Carpal tunnel syndrome can also be quite painful.[16]

Have you ever felt a little pinch in your wrists or a pain in your forearms? That comes from extensive time writing. Authors should treat their hands as though they were insured. But we neglect that area even though we use our dexterity the most.

The more time at your desk, the more you should focus on maintaining healthy hands. Pretend you're a hand model if you must, but make sure you're pampering your hands and forearms to keep them healthy. You can limit the risks of developing carpal tunnel syndrome or other pain with these tips:

- Use a wrist pad for the keyboard and mouse.
- Have your hands and forearms massaged.
- Introduce heat or cold applications.
- Take regular breaks to stretch the wrists.

Stretching Exercises for the Wrists

Using simple exercises to stretch and strengthen your wrists will help improve your range of motion. The increased flexibility can relieve pain and help you perform daily tasks more comfortably.

*Note: These general stretches can help reduce pain in the hands, wrists, and arms, but they won't directly treat carpal tunnel syndrome or other injuries. Consult your physician to ensure these stretches are safe to perform, especially if you have arthritis. Avoid stretching too far. Stop immediately if you feel any pain.

Finger stretch

- Start by placing your palm over the fingers of your opposite hand.
- Gently pull the fingers back toward your wrist, away from your palm.
- Count slowly to 25, then release.
- Perform the same stretch on the other hand.

Palm down stretch

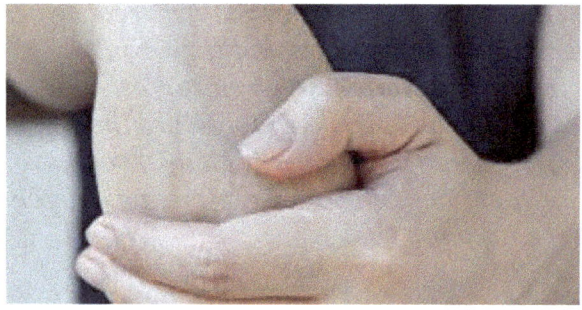

- Hold one arm straight before you, palm down.
- Bend your wrist at a 90-degree angle, pointing your fingers to the floor.

- Using your other hand, gently pull until you feel a stretch in your forearm.
- Count 15 to 30 seconds, and release.
- Stretch your other wrist the same way.
- Repeat both sides several times.

Hands together (prayer) stretch

- Place your palms together at chest height.
- Keep your hands pressed and slowly lower them toward your stomach.
- Continue lowering your hands down your body until you feel a stretch in your wrists.
- Hold for 30 seconds, then repeat

WHY YOU NEED TO KEEP YOUR PSOAS HAPPY

The psoas is not a well-known muscle, but it's so important to your body that it needs special mentioning. What's a psoas, you may ask?

The psoas is an essential muscle group acting as a primary connector between your torso and legs.

Your psoas muscle directly impacts your posture and stabilizes your spine. This muscle group is responsible for flexing your torso when you bend or moving your leg when you walk up the stairs.

The psoas muscles are not only vital to your body structure, but they also support your internal organs and your diaphragm, which directly affects your ability to walk and breathe.

See why the psoas is so important?

Because of the impact on flexion, the surrounding muscles can compensate and become overused if the psoas weakens. This can cause many of our aches and pains, including low back and pelvic pain. When the psoas is out of whack, the chain reaction of discomfort creates havoc on your already tense, stressed body.

And guess what? Prolonged bouts of sitting causes the psoas to become constantly contracted, which promotes pain and discomfort.

Stretching and releasing the tension on the psoas daily is the best way to relieve and prevent increased problems. It'll take time and consistent daily attention to keep your psoas muscles relaxed.

Here are some tips for keeping your psoas muscle happy:

1. **Avoid sitting for extended periods** – It all comes back to sitting too long and the negative impact on the body. One way to combat sitting for too long is by setting a timer reminding you to get up and move around.

Jim Stoppani, PhD, the leading authority on exercise science, sports nutrition, and supplementation, created the 30/60 Rule to combat the problem of too much sitting. Dr. Stoppani recommends after every 30 minutes of sitting consecutively to perform 60 seconds of activity.17

2. **Support your seat** – Next time you sit down to work be aware of your psoas and sit with proper posture. As mentioned in an earlier chapter, setting up your workstation is paramount to avoiding injury. As a reminder, have your hips level or slightly higher than your knees. Use a cushion and place it beneath your sit bones. This will tilt the pelvis, which relaxes the psoas. You could also place a cushion in the curve of the lower back for extra support.

3. **Try flexibility and mobility exercises** – Regular stretching sessions will do wonders to increase flexibility and mobility to relax the psoas muscle. Many basic yoga poses are a perfect match for targeting that area of the body.

4. **Get a professional massage** - Getting a massage from a knowledgeable professional can greatly relieve an angry psoas. The massage therapist has been trained to apply pressure to specific areas of the body that directly target the discomfort. They can go deep into what's called the fascia of the muscle to release the tension.

Combined with regular stretching, getting a professional massage will help your muscles relax. In fact, having a massage at least once a month is very beneficial.[18]

Renowned athlete and motivational speaker David Goggins has touted a meticulous stretching routine to stay at peak performance level. Goggins has been especially vocal on the importance of stretching the psoas muscle. He's found releasing his tight psoas with a consistent stretching regimen has been fundamental in improving his overall wellness.[19]

Stretch Out the Psoas

Glute Bridge:

- Lie on your back with your knees bent and hip-width apart
- Keep your back and bottoms of the feet flat on the ground.
- Driving through the legs and buttocks, lift your hips off the ground.
- Get as high off the ground as you can without arching the back.
- Hold for 15-30 Seconds. Lower. Repeat.

Side-Lying Psoas Stretch:

- Lie on your side with your top leg bent.
- Prop yourself up with your bottom forearm like you were doing a side-plank.
- Grab the bent leg and gently pull until your heel reaches your glutes.
- Hold the stretch for 10 seconds and do the same on the other side.

To Sum Up

The problem: Sitting Too Long

STAYING FIT WHILE YOU SIT

By now, you're beginning to realize that working at a desk or computer for long periods causes stress, fatigue, and soreness. As a result, your muscles get stiff and cause discomfort in your body and mind.

The solution: Stretch Breaks

Breaking up your workday with stretch breaks can help diminish the negative impact. If you are sitting 8, 12, 14, 16 hours or longer with no break, then you NEED to start taking this seriously.

Sample stretches

Exercise 1: Neck Stretch

- Sit upright and place your right hand on your left shoulder.
- Hold that shoulder down, and slowly tip your head toward the right.
- Keep your face pointed forward or even turned slightly toward the right.
- Hold this stretch gently for 5 seconds.
- Repeat on the other side.

Exercise 2: Shoulder Rolls

- Stand in a relaxed position with your arms at your sides.
- Shrug your shoulders up, then squeeze your shoulders back, then stretch your shoulders down, and then press them forward.

- The entire exercise should take about 7 seconds.

Exercise 3: Chair Stretch (reverse arch)

- Move to the front of the chair and interlace your fingers behind the back until your palms touch each other. (If bringing the palms together is too difficult, clasp your hands at the fingers instead).
- Take a deep breath in and let the shoulders move even further back until you feel a stretch in the chest muscles. If possible, let your head fall back to open the neck.
- Exhale all the air as you extend backwards.(Only stretch back as much as you're comfortable with.)
- Hold the position and take a few deep breaths.
- Slowly return to a normal seated position, bringing your head back up first.

Exercise 4: Figure Four or Seated Pigeon

- Keep your right leg on the floor with foot flat.
- Bend your left leg and set it across the right so that the ankle is across the right thigh. (if this is too difficult simply cross the ankles)
- Lean forward into the left leg until you feel a stretch in the back of your hip.

- Repeat the movement with the right leg atop the left.

Note: If one side feels tighter than the other spend a little more time in the stretch.

A Word on Foam Rollers

Alongside proper stretching and regular massage, using a foam roller is a great way to relieve tight muscles and stiffness. Foam rollers use your own body weight to help massage and relax your muscles. They are especially useful for finding trigger point areas that house pain, such as little knots in the muscle belly.

When foam rollers first came out, they were all the same size and shape. Now, they have been developed to meet the many different needs of the user.

There are three primary considerations when purchasing a foam roller:

Foam Roller Density

The density of a foam roller will determine how it feels. Like the fairy tale Goldilocks and the Three Bears, a roller that is too soft won't provide enough pressure on the muscles. However, if it's too dense, the roller can cause bruising, which is the opposite of what you want when foam rolling.

*Hint: The color of the roller can provide information as to its density. White foam rollers are the softest, and black the stiffest. Colors like blue or

red are typically the intermediate levels that beginners often use.

Because brands will vary, the best way to choose a foam roller is by squeezing it to assess its relative firmness.

Foam Roller Texture

The texture of foam rollers is where most of the changes have happened over the years. Foam rollers started with a smooth surface. Now you can find ridges and knobs of various sizes that offer more targeted and intense pressure.

If you're just starting with a foam roller, it's best to stick with the basic design before moving on to the textured versions.

Foam Roller Sticks

A foam roller stick is a flexible hand-held massager used similarly to traditional foam rollers. They often resemble rolling pins for baking with handles at each end and are used on the legs or upper back.

Bottom Line:

It's never too late to get started. Make a commitment to yourself and begin integrating stretches, foam rolling, regular health breaks, and proper desk set-up to reduce the negative effects of sitting and prevent further problems.

You've learned about the long-term health aspects, now discover how incorporating exercise can offset these issues. Keep reading....

4. How Exercise Affects the Body

No one ever thinks about the health risks that sitting too long can impose. But the makeup of the human body isn't meant to stay in one position for long periods. We're meant to move. Our ancestors would travel, hunt, and build, keeping them active and not allowing their physicality to stagnate.

The mental strain that accompanies a sedentary life also needs to be considered. When you're under duress all day worrying about deadlines and other stressful tasks, taking regular breaks away from your work area is important. If you allow these stressors to build on your mind and spirit all day, every day, eventually, it will take a toll on you.

Unlike other factors that have a negative impact on health, like smoking or drinking, sitting doesn't have the same stigma attached to it. We all sit at some point during the day, but the extended periods of sitting, mainly throughout the workday, are gaining attention as a risk factor for health and well-being.

The good news is you can change things by incorporating a few healthy habits and simple daily routine adjustments.

It begins with exercise, an activity that no person is too young or too old for. According to The American Heart Association, adults should get at least 150 minutes of moderate-intensity weekly activity. They also recommend moving more and sitting less to offset the health risks of being too sedentary.[20]

Engaging in physical activity boosts both your health and happiness. It significantly decreases your chances of developing cardiovascular issues and helps prevent bone deterioration. The more fit you become, the lower your risk of facing chronic diseases or injuries.

Additionally, regular exercise enhances your body's ability to burn calories by ramping up your metabolism, aiding in fat loss and weight management.

Exercise isn't just about the physical attributes either. You'll also feel a measure of stress relief due to the endorphins that are released during an exercise session.

Becoming a fitter version of yourself raises your confidence and gives you a sense of accomplishment as you attain your goals. The discipline needed to stick to an exercise routine can translate to other areas of your life, elevating you to a higher level of success.

Back when I was a competitive athlete, if I was having a bad day my trainer would always ask if I'd worked out that day. She knew how the time spent focusing on the workout and the rush of endorphins it brings would shift my sour mood.

As you can see, incorporating an exercise program into your daily life makes good sense all around.

Benefits of Exercising

Evidence suggests that our genes evolved to favor exercise. In other words, during prehistoric times, if a person couldn't move quickly and wasn't strong, that person would fall to natural predators. Those who were fit survived to reproduce and pass on their "fitter" genes through generations.

As a nationally certified personal trainer, I extensively studied how exercising impacts health and wellness. A strange thing happens when you engage in consistent exercise. Not only does it have a positive physical impact, but your emotional and mental states also lift.

Regular exercise should become part of your daily routine to fully capitalize on the benefits. It's as simple as this: do the work, reap the rewards.

That's something any author or creative can relate to. When you put the time in, you can create a masterpiece. The same is true of your physical body. This is why so many bodybuilders liken the sport to crafting a statue from clay or marble. It's an unveiling of your art, in this case, your healthiest self. That type of reveal will only come through hard work and dedication. This also includes making healthier choices for your meals, which we'll touch on later.

It's been said that "only the strong survive," but strength, combined with an intelligent approach, is the winning combination. However, the current lifestyle of most individuals is inactive and sedentary. This causes poor productivity and often leads to chronic problems.

Have you ever woken up for the day and still felt tired? Even after chugging pots of coffee, that sluggish feeling doesn't really subside. It impacts your workflow, setting you back on the completion of projects.

Think about it: how can you write in a creative flow if all you're thinking about is sleep? Brain fog won't allow you to tap into your creativity the way you need to.

The bottom line is we must start taking better care of ourselves.

Most people cringe when it comes to exercise. The first excuse is always that they don't have time. To those people, I offer you this counter: how much time do you really have to dedicate to the rest of your life? Because that's what we're talking about here.

It's less about aesthetics and more about prolonging the longevity of your life so you can enjoy every minute of it to the fullest. And honestly, if you don't focus on preventative measures now, then down the line, your poor health will be the only thing you have time for.

It's really not that time-consuming to get a proper workout, either. You'd be surprised what you can accomplish in just thirty minutes. And when you attach a strong enough reason to your goal, you'll always figure out a way to follow through on it. Whether it's bending down to pick up your child or being around long enough to walk her down the aisle, whatever drives you, then use it.

First, let's explore the different types of exercise, and then we'll discuss how you can start incorporating more activity into your day in a way that makes it challenging but still fun.

Categories of Exercise

To better understand how you can incorporate exercise into your daily life, we're going to break down the different categories of exercise and physical activities available. There are many choices out there, so anyone can find something they will enjoy doing.

Let's start today and get you on the path to a healthy lifestyle!

As we go over the different choices, you'll be able to discern for yourself which types of activities would suit you best. If it's not an enjoyable experience, you'll likely not stick with it.

You may find yourself experimenting with the different options before settling on something, and that's perfectly fine. It's important for you to look forward to the activity daily and feel energized in the pursuit of your goal.

If you're always breathing a heavy sigh because you "have to work out," then it's counter-intuitive to what you're trying to accomplish. Because this isn't a fad or a quick fix, it's a lifestyle change that you'll be making. So, if it feels like torture, try something different until you find the physical activity that's for you.

Once you get into the rhythm of training on your terms, you'll find that it becomes a healthy habit you're looking forward to as part of your day.

Exercise comes in many forms. If the weight room intimidates you, or you'd rather not be chained to a treadmill, there are still many different options available when it comes to getting your exercise in.

When you're stuck in an office for hours on end, slipping in some exercise time becomes trickier but not impossible. In the next few pages, we'll discuss how to incorporate exercise into your busy workday.

The important thing is to stay committed to getting your exercise regardless of the situation life throws at you. Your health should be your top priority. If you don't take care of yourself physically, other areas of your life will be inhibited.

Exercise is divided into three general categories:

- Aerobic
- Anaerobic
- Flexibility

A balanced program should include all three.

What is Aerobic Exercise?

Aerobic exercise includes any activity that gets your heart racing and boosts your oxygen intake.

Doing these kinds of workouts can really help your heart, lungs, and overall circulation.

The American Heart Association suggests aiming for at least 150 minutes of moderate aerobic exercise each week. To make the most of your fitness routine, try to gradually increase how long and intense your workouts are, spreading them throughout the week for the best results.[21]

Benefits of Aerobic Exercise[21]

- Improves cardiovascular health
- Lowers blood pressure
- Aids sleep
- Regulates weight
- Strengthens immune system
- Improves brain power
- Boosts mood

WHAT IS ANAEROBIC TRAINING?

Anaerobic training encompasses various forms of exercise aimed at enhancing muscle mass, endurance, and functional strength. This includes a variety of techniques like bodyweight exercises, functional workouts, and weight training, which can be performed with either machines or free weights.

Benefits of Anaerobic Training[22]

- Makes you stronger
- Burns calories efficiently
- Decreases abdominal fat

- Can help you appear leaner
- Decreases your risk of falls
- Lowers your risk of injury
- Improves mental health
- Makes your bones stronger
- Promotes a better quality of life

WHAT IS FLEXIBILITY TRAINING?

Your body gets stiff from sitting all day. By adding in stretching routines, it can make your body more flexible and supple. Being flexible helps you to move smoothly without limitations. By incorporating flexibility exercises daily, you'll gain a better range of motion, improved balance, and reduce the risk of injury. The benefits of increased flexibility can significantly impact your overall health and wellness.

Benefits of Flexibility[23]

- Fewer injuries
- Less pain
- Improved posture and balance
- Greater range of motion
- Improved physical performance

As you can see, there are multiple benefits to engaging in regular exercise. It's not just about how you look but how you feel. Instead of shunning exercise as a chore, envision it as the antidote to the stress, pain, and silent killers plaguing your body. That's not to say that exercise is a cure-all for every ailment, but the benefits outweigh the excuses at this point. Don't you think?

Now that you know how exercise positively impacts the body, it's time to learn how to incorporate it into your daily routine. As a reminder, check with your physician before you begin any new form of exercise.

The following section will show you how to do the work even when you lack the time or the drive.

These sample workouts and ideas aren't meant to prepare you to compete on a bodybuilding stage. I'll say it again: This is NOT about aesthetics; this is about developing whole body health to feel your best. Having a leaner, more toned body due to your hard work is just icing on the cake!

It's time to get serious about your health and fitness! These easy, actionable tips will help you get started....

5. The Workouts

When we sit at a desk hunched over a computer all day typing out the Great American Novel, our bodies are in a state of flexion. This means the body is bent, and the muscles are contracted, leading to bad posture and muscle imbalances.

As a result, this causes poor movement patterns and, eventually, chronic pain or worse. In other words, the body remembers these patterns and locks the muscles. It's like getting a memory foam pillow. After using it for a few nights, the pillow shapes to the weight and structure of your head.

Like the pillow, our bodies will bounce back, until it can do it no longer.

To offset this, we need to move more through strength training, flexibility exercises, cardiovascular fitness, and mobility work to restore proper alignment to the body. But even if you factor in a solid workout each day, that still may not be enough to offset the damage from sitting.

So, how do we conquer, or at least curb, the effects of a sedentary lifestyle? The answer is: "fitness breaks."

Do you ever see the people in your office taking 5 to 6 smoke breaks during their workday? Or maybe you smoke, and you're out there puffing away on a cigarette multiple times a day. I'm not here to judge or to lecture you on the health risks of smoking.

My point is that the same amount of time put into smoke breaks can be used instead for "fitness breaks." These are small doses of activity performed throughout the day that can be done right from your desk or office space. Implementing "fitness breaks" will make you feel a lot better than daily smoking or vaping. And you won't even need a change of clothes!

As mentioned in an earlier chapter, Dr. Jim Stoppani recommends the 30/60 rule. For every 30 minutes you sit, you'll engage in 60 seconds of activity.[17] This could be running in place, taking a brisk walk, or even bodyweight squats at your desk.

Later in this section, I'll discuss specific ways to incorporate activity during your workday.

Adding fitness breaks and following the 30/60 rule is a simple and effective way to maintain or improve your health. During most of these workouts, you'll simply use your body weight. For others, resistance bands or small dumbbells are recommended. These items can easily be stored at your desk or in a gym bag.

The intent is to get the blood flowing, engage the muscle fibers, and energize the body. ***Now, LFG!***

THROWING YOUR BODY WEIGHT AROUND

Using your body weight is one of the most effective ways of exercising, especially when you have limited resources, such as working in an office, consistently traveling, or as a commercial driver on the road.

Body weight exercises are also very beneficial for beginners as they help you learn how to control your body during each movement without having the concern or stress of added weight placed upon you. Working out with your own body weight tests your coordination, flexibility, balance, and strength. If you can't move around your own body weight, you shouldn't be trying to pick up a dumbbell or barbell yet.

Not only are bodyweight exercises a great way to work the entire body, but they're also free. As a plus, your body is always with you wherever you go!

Say you travel to a lot of writers conferences, and the hotel doesn't have a gym, or you don't have time for a complete workout. You can easily do a quick bodyweight circuit right in your hotel room. You'll blast that jet lag off you and be energized for any literary meetings or panels that await you that day.

So, there's really no more excuses. You've got all the tools you need at your disposal. Here are a few sample bodyweight exercises to get you started:

- SQUATS
- LUNGES
- PUSHUPS
- DIPS
- PLANKS
- CRUNCHES

STAYING FIT WHILE YOU SIT

- LEG RAISES

These are all standard bodyweight exercises that you've no doubt seen or even tried before. You can do these exercises separately or pair them together in a circuit.

For example, if we go back to the 30/60 rule from Dr. Jim, you'd get up from your seat after 30 minutes of work and pick an exercise from the list to perform for 60 seconds.

Set a timer as a reminder and just get started. Keep it fun by switching up which exercise you choose for your breaks. You'll be amazed at how soon it becomes your new standard for the day. If 60 seconds seems too daunting, scale it back to a time that suits you. But I would recommend not going under 20 seconds.

After a while, you can bump up the time if you want to. Start to incorporate some of the stretches mentioned in the last chapter. The goal is to get you up and moving around. However you want to incorporate that, it's up to you. Just don't back out on your plan. It takes very little to break up the stagnation of sitting. You'll feel much better if you do.

Note: I recognize there are some with specialized needs. For those, I would suggest speaking with your doctor about how to incorporate fitness activities that suit your situation.

Can't Resist the Resistance Bands

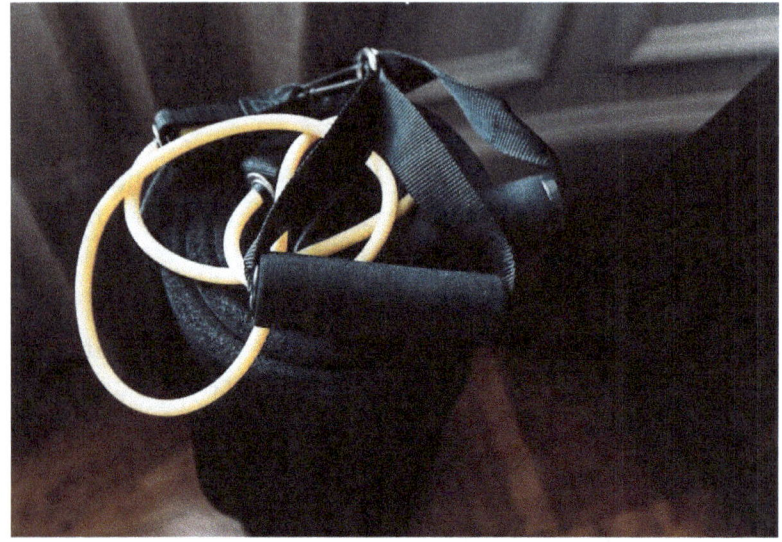

Resistance bands are a training tool that can be used for both strength training and cardiovascular health. They resemble rubber tubing with handles but pack a healthy punch similar to dumbbells.

While exercising is an integral part of being healthy, getting stronger, and preventing injury, that doesn't always mean you have to be in a gym. Resistance bands are lightweight and easy to carry, making them portable enough to bring to the office or on a work trip. You can even hang them up in your workspace or stick them in a drawer for easy access.

The bands come in different weight sizes, allowing you to progress in your training (more on that later), and they put little to no pressure on your joints, making them a great tool for beginning to intermediate workouts.

Resistance bands can be used to work your entire body to improve your strength, flexibility, and posture. They can also be incorporated into stretching routines to increase the range of movement. This helps prevent and alleviate neck, shoulders, back, hips, and knee pain.

When you use resistance bands, consistent tension is maintained while lifting and lowering during the exercise. You'll completely control the resistance load, eliminating the risk of taking on too much before you're ready. This makes resistance bands a great option for many people.

To help you get the most from your resistance bands, here are a few of the exercises you can perform directly at your desk:

Resistance Band Bicep Curl

Step on the resistance band so it is centered on the bottom of your foot. To apply more resistance, use both feet. Hold one handle in each hand, arms extended, palms facing out.

Keeping your elbows tight at the sides of your body, slowly curl your hands up toward your shoulders. Squeeze your biceps at the top of the movement, then slowly lower your hands to the starting position. Repeat for 10-15 reps.

Resistance Band Upright Row

Stand with one or both feet on the middle of the resistance band. Hold one handle in each hand, arms in front of your body, palms facing towards you with the band equal length on both sides.

With your back straight and abs tight, slowly lift your hands until they reach shoulder height. Your elbows should flare out to the sides as if you're pouring a pitcher of water. Slowly lower your hands back to the starting position. Repeat for 10-15 reps.

Resistance Band Row

Loop the band around a sturdy post and hold each of the handles, palms facing each other. Step back until the band is taut, which will give you enough resistance throughout the movement.

Bend your elbows, pulling the band towards you until it reaches your torso. Squeeze your shoulder blades together, then slowly straighten your arms back to the starting position. Repeat for 10-15 reps.

Resistance Band Chest Press

Loop the resistance band around a stable support. Turn away from the band and grasp the handles so they're directly under your armpits. Step one foot forward to increase the tension in the band.

Slowly press both hands forward, palms facing the ground, until your arms are fully extended. Squeeze your chest and then slowly return to the start position. This exercise mimics a standard cable chest press you would see in any gym set-up. Repeat for 10-15 reps.

DUMBBELLS BY THE DESK

Dumbbells have been a staple of workout routines for many years. This is because you can attack the entire body from a variety of angles using just a set of dumbbells. They also ensure balance if one side is more dominant during lifts.

They come in a wide range of weight sizes, but for these workouts, you really don't need to go too heavy. The intent is to use a set of dumbbells for a quick lifting session and then get back to work. If you're heading into a gym for a longer workout, you'll want to research proper form and technique.

Right now, we're just getting you up from your chair and doing a burst of activity. Stick with a weight that you can comfortably lift for 10 – 15 repetitions (aka reps).

These are some of the standard dumbbell exercises that work the largest muscles in the body. Remember to warm up thoroughly before performing any of these lifts. That can be as simple as a few arm circles or bodyweight squats. Any type of movement to warm up the joints and muscles. Just don't go into a lift cold, and remember to keep the weight light.

We're not trying to impress anyone with ego lifts; we're trying to get you healthier and more active!

Bent-Over Double Dumbbell Row

Slightly bend your knees and hinge at the hips so your upper torso is parallel to the floor. Holding a dumbbell in each hand, palms facing each other, pull the weight up towards you until the dumbbell is level with your ribcage.

Squeeze your shoulder blades, hold the contraction for a second, and then return to the starting position. Keep your abs and glutes tight and back straight throughout the exercise. Focus on pulling with your back rather than your arms. Repeat for 10-15 reps.

Dumbbell Deadlift

Hold a pair of dumbbells with an overhand grip at arm's length in front of your thighs. Keep your feet hip-width apart, knees slightly bent, hinge at the hips, and lower your torso until the dumbbells reach mid-shin level. Pause, then raise your torso back to the starting position, focusing on squeezing your buttocks muscle. This movement should be slow and controlled throughout. Do not rush! Repeat for 10-15 reps.

Squat

Start by standing shoulder-width apart. Grab a dumbbell in each hand and keep them close to your sides, palms facing your hips. Bend the knees as though you're sitting in a chair until the thighs are parallel to the ground. Pause for three seconds before standing back into the starting position.

Important note: Keep the back from rounding throughout the movement.

Dumbbell Lunge

Holding a pair of dumbbells, arms at your sides, take a step forward and lower your back knee as close to the floor as possible. For safety, keep the knee of your front leg from going past your toes. Push back through the heels to a standing position.

Using a controlled pace, alternate your steps. You can keep your arms at your sides throughout the workout or add a dumbbell curl with each step forward.

If you don't have enough space or don't want to walk up and down the halls of your office, you can do stationary lunges instead. This means that instead of walking, you'll lunge forward, step back into place, and then step forward with the other leg.

Dumbbell Shoulder Press

With a focus on the shoulder muscles, the dumbbell shoulder press can be done while sitting in your chair or standing. Hold a dumbbell in each hand at shoulder level, palms facing away from you. Keep your chest up and abs tight, and press the weights up until your arms are straight above your head. Slowly return to the starting position, keeping your elbows out to the sides and bent at a 90-degree angle.

Important note: If you feel any sharp pain while performing these exercises, stop immediately and consult your physician.

How to Get in Your Cardio

I've discussed the benefits of cardiovascular work in earlier chapters. To reiterate, cardio is a necessity for building heart health and endurance. It also helps strip the body of stored fat to see the lean muscle mass you've built through your strength training workouts.

When you're in an office environment, you're not going to want to get a full sweat on while wearing business attire or even when it's casual Friday. If you're writing your novel at the home office, pausing in the middle of a flow isn't convenient either. But there are ways in which you can turn on your cardio engine without the need to jump on a treadmill.

These quick bursts of cardiovascular exercise can be done at your workstation in short sprints or circuits:

- JUMPING JACKS
- JUMPING SQUATS
- JUMP LUNGES
- RUN IN PLACE
- SHADOW BOXING

- SKIERS

Introducing bursts of movement throughout the day wakes the body up. The heart starts pumping, blood flows, and you become more energized. With more energy, your productivity increases.

Think of it like an attic that is filled with dust and clutter. It's dark, dank, and not much light gets in. Then, one day, you decide to clean out the attic. The junk is cleared away, the dust is wiped, and the windows are open to let the sunlight in.

Shaking up your system with a burst of cardio is like opening those windows. Now, things are clearer, and you can get back to work with renewed vigor.

Remember that plot hole you were stuck on? You just needed a jolt of energy to help you plow through it!

Most people hit a 2pm slump and reach for the coffee. Caffeine is a quick-fix method that doesn't always have the desired effect. The reason for the afternoon slump is often the result of a fluctuating metabolism (more on that later).

Introducing caffeine is like jumping a bad battery in a car. The charge only lasts for a little while until another jump is needed. It's better to replace the battery rather than jump the car repeatedly.

There is a misconception that you'll be tired after a workout, but the opposite is true. Energy from the endorphins released during exercise will propel you much longer than a coffee loaded with sugar and fatty creamers.

So, the next time you feel sluggish during the day get up and do a quick thirty seconds of jumping jacks or jog in place. You'd be surprised at the results!

Opening the Mind and Body with Yoga

When you hear the word yoga, does it drum up a certain image or preconceived notion? As a former powerlifter who focused mostly on strength training, I used to put flexibility to the side as I focused on lifting weights. After stepping away from that career, I started to learn the immense benefits of practicing yoga.

Yoga can improve strength, balance, and flexibility. The practice uses deep breathing techniques and postural movements designed to stretch the muscles and improve blood flow. This technique can ease the stiffness that comes from sitting all day.

Like most workouts, yoga can be scaled to meet your needs. You can even drop a yoga mat next to your desk and practice some poses during your workday.

If you work from home, it's a bit easier to roll out your yoga mat and stretch out. At an office, it can be a bit trickier, but not entirely out of the question. In fact, you don't even have to get up from your chair to benefit from yoga poses.

The Benefits of Chair Yoga

Doing yoga from your chair allows you to stay seated while practicing yoga-focused poses. Chair yoga offers similar benefits to traditional yoga but removes some of the challenges.24 For instance, if you have trouble balancing, using a chair for yoga poses can help stabilize you until the muscles get stronger.

Yoga benefits, whether in a chair or not, can include improved muscle tone, better breathing habits, stress reduction,25 better sleep, and an improved sense of well-being.26 Not to mention, the stretches will help counteract the day's stiffness.

Doing yoga from your chair is all about adaptability. You want to be able to go right into a flow from your desk. So, the style of chair you use doesn't matter. However, if your chair has wheels, that won't work unless the wheels can be locked.

Try one of these chair yoga sequences the next time you feel stiff. Remember to go at your own pace and maintain good posture as you move through the motion.

Chair Cat Arch-Cat Lift

- Sit up straight with your feet flat on the floor. Set your hands on your knees or the tops of your thighs.
- Inhale and arch your spine until your shoulder blades are close to touching. This is the cat arch position.

- Exhale and let your chin drop to your chest, letting your shoulders roll forward. This is the cat lift position.
- Continue moving between the arch and lift positions on each breath.

Chair Raised Hands Pose

- Assume a neutral posture, ensuring that your spine is elongated and your shoulders are at ease.
- Inhale deeply while elevating your arms towards the ceiling until you experience a stretch in the shoulder and upper back regions.
- Upon exhalation, lower your arms into a prayer position at the center of your chest.
- Continue to repeat this sequence, maintaining a harmonious connection between your breath and each movement.

Chair Forward Bend

- As you exhale, transition into a forward bend, allowing your torso to fold over your legs.
- If possible, place your hands on the ground, and allow your head to hang down, feeling the weight of it.
- Upon inhalation, lift your arms back up overhead.
- Continue to alternate between the raised arm position and the forward bend multiple

times, synchronizing your movements with your breath.

Chair Extended Side Angle

- Bend forward and maintain the position through the movement.
- Position your left fingertips on the ground outside your left foot. If your left hand struggles to reach the floor, consider using a block for support or resting it on your left knee, allowing for a twist from that position.
- As you inhale, expand your chest while twisting to the right, raising your right arm and directing your gaze toward the ceiling. Hold this position for several breaths before lowering the right arm on an exhale.
- Repeat the same alignment with the right arm lowered and the left arm elevated.

Chair Pigeon

- Sit tall. Place your right ankle on your left thigh, making sure your knee is as aligned with your ankle as possible.
- Hold this position for three to five breaths.
- If you wish, lean forward to deepen the stretch.
- Switch to your left leg and repeat the same steps.

Chair Spinal Twist

- Sit sideways on the chair, facing left. Rotate your torso to the left while gripping the back of the chair to perform a spinal twist.
- As you inhale, lengthen your spine, and as you exhale, deepen the twist for five breaths.
- Shift your legs to the right side of the chair and repeat the twist to the right.

Making Mobility Matter

You've heard me talk about flexibility throughout this guide. But mobility is just as important for overall wellness. The two terms go hand-in-hand, but they actually have different benefits. Understanding how they differ will help you when trying to maximize your mobility.

Differences between mobility and flexibility

Mobility refers to how well you can move your joints and how unrestricted your movement feels. In contrast, flexibility is more about how your muscles, ligaments, and tendons can stretch without any tightness. Mobility is all about dynamic movements, while flexibility is usually linked to static stretches. To improve both, you can try stretching, yoga, cardio exercises, and strength training.

Why is mobility important?

Having good mobility is important for many reasons. If you can't move well, your joints can get stiff, making everyday activities like sitting, standing, and walking much harder. In fact, poor mobility can increase the risk of getting injured.

For instance, someone who struggles with knee or ankle mobility might be more prone to falls. Plus, poor mobility can lead to physical decline and make people dependent on others as they age.

How to Improve Mobility

Recognizing the importance of mobility is just the first step; the next important task is to find ways to improve it. This is especially important as we age and start to lose mobility. The fluid in the joints decreases as we get older, which leads to stiffness and less movement. The elasticity of our connective tissues also tends to decline, which further restricts flexibility.

Besides aging, many factors can affect a person's mobility and flexibility. Genetics, past injuries or surgeries, muscle imbalances, and posture all contribute to how well someone can move.

Mobility exercises focus on improving movement patterns, joint function, and overall capability. These dynamic movements help prepare the body for specific activities. Mobility stretches focus on improving movement and effectively controlling various muscle groups, joints, and connective tissues. They also enhance the body's ability to strengthen and stabilize as it moves in different directions.

Based on all the sitting I do as a writer, coupled with heavy weight lifting, I started to feel a lot of muscular tightness. My lower back, shoulders, and especially my hips were very stiff after several hours of work. It was only when I started doing regular mobility movements that I saw improvements. More importantly, I felt better.

I began doing specific movement patterns daily, targeting my hips, back, and upper shoulders. Integrating these moves for just a few minutes in the morning and before bed has helped me reduce pain and stiffness. The important thing is to introduce specific movements to target your areas of discomfort.

Nutrition is equally important, as the body requires specific nutrients and enough hydration to maintain its mobility. For instance, collagen is essential for healthy connective tissues, while calcium and vitamin D contribute to the health of bones and joints.

Nutrition truly affects many aspects of your body. The upcoming chapter will focus on maintaining good nutrition, even when juggling a hectic work schedule.

6. Knowing Your Nutrition

Even the most solid workout plan needs to be backed by proper nutrition for the best health results. And let's face it, one of the other major problems of a sedentary job or lifestyle is poor nutritional habits. These habits are picked up over time until they become a ritual you run on autopilot.

The problem usually starts first thing in the morning. Most people are in a rush to start work, so they often skip breakfast. If your main job is being a full-time author, congratulations! However, even without the commute to work you'll likely run into your own problems.

Maybe you've got a household to run. Which means, you're responsible for getting everyone else ready for school or work and out the door on time.

Whatever the case, breakfast is skipped, and that's not a good thing. Missing breakfast can make you feel sluggish, mess with your focus, and even spark cravings that throw off your healthy eating for the rest of the day.

Why Breakfast Matters

Breakfast is often called the most important meal of the day, and there's a good reason for that. The food we eat in the morning significantly influences our energy levels and overall health throughout the day. If we skip breakfast, it may slow our metabolism, sap our energy, give us brain fog, and increase the likelihood of overeating later.

Starting your day with a well-balanced breakfast has multiple benefits:[27]

Fires Up Your Metabolism

While you sleep, your body is fasting. When you wake up, it's ready to have that nourishment replaced. That's why it's called "breakfast," because you break your fast. Having a balanced meal first thing in the morning will regulate blood sugar levels and jumpstart your metabolism.

*Note: I'm aware of intermittent fasting and how many people opt to skip breakfast to adhere to their fasting schedule. That's not what my guide is about. I've tried IF myself, and I didn't like what it did to my blood sugar.

IF is an advanced technique used by athletes. It's important to understand exactly what it entails before you just start skipping meals. It's about shifting your calorie intake, not just skipping breakfast to magically cut pounds. Plus, females need to be aware of how intermittent fasting can impact their hormones. I'm not going to get into all of that in this guide.

There are many medical professionals who you can seek out that will explain the benefits and possible side effects of doing intermittent fasting.

Don't just pick it up from your favorite social media influencer. Do actual research before making intermittent fasting a part of your nutritional plan.

Enhances Mental Focus and Performance

Your brain needs nutrients to function the way it's supposed to. Having breakfast provides glucose, which boosts memory and overall clarity. Skipping breakfast can leave you with "brain fog," making it harder to concentrate and leave you feeling fatigued, which can affect your productivity.

Improves Mood and Emotional Well-Being

Breakfast is a mood booster. Meaning when you start the day with nutrient-dense foods, it supplies the brain with essential vitamins and minerals (as noted above). This helps to regulate serotonin and dopamine, which are responsible for emotional well-being. However, if you skip breakfast, it can cause fluctuating blood sugar levels, which leads to irritability and mood swings.

Regulates Hunger and Prevents Overeating

Starting your morning with a balance of protein and fiber will keep your hunger regulated throughout the day. The sensation of fullness will keep you from reaching for calorie-loaded snacks and cause you to overeat during lunch. By eating breakfast, you'll stay fuller for longer and minimize those energy slumps.

In every office I've worked in, someone brought bagels or donuts as an office treat. They're portable, come in many flavors, and you can get enough for the entire office without breaking the bank. They're also full of sugars and simple carbohydrates, which should be avoided. But this is often not the case, especially if you've skipped breakfast. Your body craves nutrients, so you indulge and have "just one."

What happens now is you'll get a temporary sugar high that will wear off quickly, resulting in a blood-sugar crash and leaving you sluggish. You'll likely reach for a caffeine fix to boost your energy levels. But you won't do your body any favors if you load your coffee with extra sugar and heavy creamers.

The problem is compounded when the workload piles up and you don't take a proper lunch. Instead, you grab a quick and greasy option from a drive-thru window and either eat in the car or at the desk while continuing to work.

This situation often leads to heightened stress and digestive issues. By the end of your workday, you may feel drained, bloated, and lacking the motivation to cook, prompting you to choose quick and easy options again.

At times, the workload can get so overwhelming that meals are completely sacrificed. When you don't eat regularly, it can affect your blood sugar levels, which impacts your energy. Low blood sugar can leave you tired, dizzy, sluggish, and shaky.

Additionally, it may be difficult to concentrate if your brain doesn't get the essential fuel it needs.28 As writers, we rely on our brainpower to tap into our creativity. If you can't think clearly, how are you going to write well?

Relying on snacks to fuel your day is a quick-fix option. But when you eat nothing but small snacks throughout your day, you wind up overindulging after work because your body is craving nutrients. This can lead to a binge session which then spikes your blood sugar and causes a crash.

A similar scenario can play out even if you work from home. We get so caught up in our work that we forget to eat. Then, the cycle of poor nutrition choices begins. It becomes easier to reach for a snack and a soda while you're writing rather than getting up to cook a meal.

The key to avoiding this cycle is to make better choices in advance. You want to have balanced meals throughout the day to keep you full and satisfied without sugar spikes or bloating.

Avoiding Caffeine Crash

Do you find yourself feeling sluggish and irritable as the day goes by? Grabbing a third cup of coffee or a large soda with lunch isn't going to help. Drinking large quantities of caffeine to feel energized often has the opposite effect. While coffee may give you a boost earlier in the morning, it fades later that same day and you experience a "caffeine crash."

What is a caffeine crash?

Coffee, sodas, tea, or energy drinks are widely consumed in any workplace. I know Hollywood likes to portray writers as drunks, but the drink of choice for most of us is coffee, not booze. In other parts of the world, people prefer to drink tea. There's just something about having a hot cup of something by your computer as you write your novel.

Regardless of how you get your caffeine fix, it gets metabolized by the body faster than you might think. The energy-boosting effects only last between three to five hours. Sometimes that caffeine kick will last longer for those who metabolize it slower.

Every individual is unique, which means that people react to caffeine in different ways. As a natural stimulant, caffeine energizes the central nervous system so you feel more alert and focused. But, as the caffeine wears off, many individuals experience a caffeine crash.

Side effects can vary but often include drowsiness, irritability, and difficulty concentrating. This is the exact opposite of what you want your caffeine drink to do. When your side effects are similar to a hangover with stomach discomfort and light sensitivity[29], it's time to make a change.

How to Eliminate a Caffeine Crash

Moderation is key when it comes to anything indulgent. Caffeine is no exception. If you depend on that morning stimulant to power you through the day, you might not get that same caffeine jolt over time.

However, quitting caffeine abruptly can lead to some uncomfortable withdrawal symptoms. It's better to gradually wean yourself from the caffeine you consume.

That's not to say that coffee or tea are all bad for you. But I recommend you stay away from soda as it holds no redeeming nutritional value. On the other hand, coffee and tea do have health benefits when consumed in moderation.

A good approach is having no more than two cups of coffee daily. The caffeine in tea will depend on the type and brewing method. For instance, Matcha green tea is very high in caffeine while regular green tea is around 45mg per 8-ounce cup. Use your discretion.

The rest of the time, drink water!

WHY WATER IS SO IMPORTANT

Let's take a minute to talk about water. Be honest with yourself, are you drinking enough water every day? You may think that the solitary glass you have is sufficient, but you'd be surprised.

Most people are drinking far less water than they should be. And the lack of water can take its toll on your overall health. Couple that with the amount of coffee and soft drinks consumed (as I mentioned in the previous section) and there's a serious risk of dehydration.

Have you ever been dehydrated? I mean, to the point where your body feels ill? I have, and it's not a fun experience. In fact, I'd take the worst type of flu over severe dehydration any day. You don't want to wind up in that situation. It's honestly very dangerous.

Our bodies are made up of 60% water, which needs to be replenished to stay healthy and functioning properly. Staying hydrated has plenty of other benefits, too. Drinking enough water throughout the day can help you to lose weight!

How you ask? Often, we think we're hungry, and we go for a snack or a full meal, thinking we need to eat. The truth is that, often, the body is dehydrated, not hungry. Drinking water replenishes your body, causing the cravings to dissipate. You'll feel a sense of fullness, and you'll no longer want to eat.

Ensuring you're getting enough water will also stave off the brain fog that comes with dehydration. You'll think better and be more productive with your day. Water also keeps the skin supple and looking fresh.[30]

Imagine all the positive benefits that come just from drinking water!

How Much Water to Drink?

So, how much water do you need to drink each day? There's so much information out there that it can get a little confusing. As you age, you won't feel as thirsty, and this can cause you to drink much less than your body needs. According to the Mayo Clinic, the current recommendation is to drink 3.7 liters of water for men and 2.7 liters for women.[31]

An easy reminder is to drink a full glass of water with each meal. As you increase your activity level with exercise, you'll also want to increase your water intake. Ideally, you should be sipping water throughout your entire day. This is where getting a thermos comes in handy. I like to fill mine at the start of the day and set it on my desk as a reminder.

Having the thermos right in front of you will remind you to take consistent sips throughout the day. Away from the office, you should keep a glass of water by your bedside. The first thing you do when you wake up is drink the entire thing. You'll start your day off right as the water activates your body like an "on" switch.

Keep track of your water intake for a few weeks until it becomes second nature. Get a thermos with measurements on the side of it, or else mark it yourself so you know how much you've been drinking throughout the day. Set some goals to follow so you're more likely to stick to drinking enough. Make it a game, include others, and have some fun with it!

Anything you need to do to stick to your goals is encouraged.

Pack Your Snacks

There's a thing our animal friends do throughout the day called grazing. Out in the field, cows and horses will munch on grass or bits of hay continuously. They have an intrinsic knowledge of their digestive systems and they answer the signals sent out to snack.

Eating all day might seem counter-intuitive to losing weight but eating a small meal or snack every three to four hours boosts your metabolism, keeps you satisfied, maintains your energy and sugar levels, and reduces hunger cravings. But it's not just about eating every few hours to get the best results; the trick is eating the right snacks.

Most of the time the easy fix is to grab foods loaded with sugar and rich carbohydrates like donuts, bagels, or chips. Instead, add good fats and lean protein such as hard-boiled eggs, string cheese, and fruit. Snacks that pack in plenty of protein are the best option to keep you full and sustained.

The protein will keep you feeling fuller for longer as the food is digested more slowly. This eliminates sugar crashes, powers your metabolism, and keeps you feeling sated, so you don't make unhealthy choices come lunchtime.

Snack ideas to get you started:

- MIXED NUTS
- BELL PEPPER WITH GUACAMOLE
- APPLE SLICES WITH NUT BUTTER
- MIXED BERRIES IN GREEK YOGURT

- COTTAGE CHEESE WITH FLAXSEEDS
- CELERY WITH CREAM CHEESE
- CARROT SLICES WITH HUMMUS
- HARD-BOILED EGGS

Take Home Message

Sometimes you just really need a snack. I've had situations arise where I've eaten a hearty breakfast, yet a few hours later I get hungry. As you start adding exercise to your day, don't be surprised if you start getting hungrier. This is a good thing! It means your metabolism is firing and burning calories, so your body is looking to replace them. Having some healthy and nutritious options close by can help you avoid unhealthy and fattening alternatives.

MAKE TIME FOR LUNCH

When was the last time you took a real lunch break? You know, one where you got up from your desk and sat somewhere else; where you weren't using your left hand to eat your sandwich and your right hand on the mouse to finish up that spreadsheet; where you actually savored every bite of your food, instead of shoving forkfuls of salad into your mouth while staring at a computer screen.

Sandwiches over Snacks

I can't stress this enough: you have a lunch hour, use it! I've seen so many people eat at their desks, or not even eat at all, just to get through their workload.

This isn't healthy and, in the end, it will detract from your productivity.

This entire guide is predicated on the fact that you need to step away from the desk to combat the health risks that stem from sitting too long. It's also a sanity saver. If you're too long in the seat trying to tackle a project or a problem, your mind is going to go haywire. Once those delicate circuits in your mind fry, they'll shut down and you guessed it, burn out! Then who is going to finish your novel?

It's better to take a few minutes to step away, refuel your body with some much-needed nutrients and down time, then go back to the task after you're recharged.

Grinding yourself into the ground trying to check an imaginary box that says "complete" is counter-intuitive. The truth is you're not going to be complete. As long as there is work to be done, you'll continue to be busy. That's true of working for a company or working for yourself.

This can become especially hazardous if you're an entrepreneur or an author. We've already discussed how these vocations can tend to bring on even longer and harder working sessions. In fact, the writer's motto is "butt in chair, hands on keys." These days it's a badge of honor to crank out a large word count or a novel every three months. But how much of that is usable in the long run?

If you're in a flow, I get it. You want to tap into your creative genius before it fizzles out and your Muse leaves you. But don't get so wrapped up in the task in front of you that you disregard your health over it.

STAYING FIT WHILE YOU SIT

We can put a lot of pressure on ourselves trying to come up with the perfect novel. And I for one have gotten overwhelmed by self-imposed deadlines. But perfection doesn't exist. Chasing it is a waste of time and energy.

High-level executives or executive assistants are guilty of this quite a bit. They fear that if they don't finish the project by a certain time they'll be chastised or even fired over it.

Remember this: It's your right to take a lunch break. Hell, in most states it's required by law that you get two 10-minute breaks and a full hour for lunch. If an employer had their way, they'd keep you chained to that desk until everything for the day was handled.

But you're not a robot, you're a human being and your health should always come first regardless of the job. I cannot stress this enough!

Just remember: **"You're killing yourself for a job that would replace you in a week if you dropped dead."**

If you're working for yourself, that's a little harder to digest. But if you dropped dead, or got sick, because you worked yourself into the ground, who would step in and take over for you? You're the one who has the vision to build your business or write your book. No one is going to do it for you, and no one is going to tell you to take a break.

You have to be accountable for yourself.

Sometimes it's during a lunch session, when your mind can focus, that you get some of your brightest and best ideas. Fantasy author Brandon Sanderson has it worked into his daily writing routine to stop and get some exercise no matter what. He uses that time to refocus his mind on his writing.

Breaks are important. Don't neglect a proper lunch break.

Research indicates that only around 20% of American employees actually take a proper lunch break. Although it might appear to be a luxury in the current work culture, nutrition and workplace productivity experts argue that it is essential for health and job performance.

Here's why:

Less Likely to Overeat

You're not juggling tasks when you're not busy with work while eating. This can help you focus on what you're eating and how much, which can prevent you from overeating.

There's a common idea that it takes about 20 minutes for your brain and stomach to communicate and realize you're full. So, if you're rushing through your meal while distracted by work, you might eat more than you would if you took the time to be present in the moment.

So, slow down and enjoy your lunch!

Replenish Your Mental Energy

Mental energy is limited for everyone. It's crucial for staying focused, managing our actions, being creative, and making important choices. However, using up all that mental energy during the day can wear us out.

Your mind is like a muscle. The more you work it, the stronger it gets, but it also needs time to recover.

The longer we push through without a break, the more our energy levels drop, making everything feel harder. Taking a lunch break helps to recharge those energy reserves.

Help to Prevent Burnout

Your decisions today can impact the way you feel later on. You might think taking a proper lunch break is minor, but it's important enough to affect your health and wellness. Sure, people can push through for a while without taking breaks, but that's not a sustainable way to go. Eventually, it'll catch up to you, leading to stress, burnout, and unhappiness.

It's an Opportunity to Recharge (Especially If Your Book Is Dragging)

Grab your favorite sandwich and sit at the table to eat it. Or go across the street to the park and get some fresh air with your lunch. Whatever you do, step away from the computer screen while you eat.

This will help you gain more clarity on the novel you're writing, especially if you've been struggling with a part of it. Making time for lunch and returning with fresh eyes and a full stomach will help you re-channel your energy into the story.

It's Also an Opportunity to Move

This entire guide is about staying fit while you sit. And I've explained how if you spend your days glued to a desk it will cause problems down the road.

As discussed, the eye strain and back pain can add up. That's why getting up from your workstation during lunch is especially important. If you're stuck in your chair all day, you're not just dealing with tired eyes and a sore back but also piling on mental fatigue. Plus, research supports moving around during your lunch break to boost your mood and even ramp up your enthusiasm for the rest of the day.

Food is many things, but mainly, it's meant to be enjoyed and appreciated. It's also our fuel to power through the day. If you're skipping lunch or treating mealtime like a chore to squeeze in at your desk, how much are you tuning into your body and its needs?

Skip the Drive Through

It would be very easy to grab a quick burger from the clown's head or some chicken in a bucket, but as convenient as these options are, they're contributing to trouble later.

I know that fast food options are on every corner peddling their wares like drug dealers. It's hard to resist, especially if you've fallen into a pattern of going through the drive-thru regularly. Again, it's a matter of trying to save time on lunch and eat something quick so you can get back to work.

Those options are quick because they're not cooked in a healthy manner. I don't care how many gluten-free, meat-free labels they want to put on their menus. The bottom line is in the ingredients and cooking methods.

Most of the time, you'll find sugar and a high amount of salt in these meals. Yes, those fries you're addicted to are addicting for a reason. They have sugar cooked in them. Sugar turns to fat, and well, fat clogs your arteries and gives you a heart attack in your thirties if you're not careful!

As much as the fast food industry has tried to offer healthy options, they still aren't doing you as much good as cooking for yourself.

What's the Deal with Meal Prepping?

When I suggest cooking for yourself, the worry of time, or lack thereof, comes up again. But meal prepping is very simple. All it takes is setting aside a dedicated day when you'll make the bulk of your meals for the week.

Meal prepping is well known in bodybuilding circles, but it easily translates into everyday life. When you meal prep, you make your meals in advance of the work week before you get too busy. Most of the time that falls on a Sunday, with Monday being the start of a new work week, but you can choose any day you prefer.

On that chosen day, you'll make your meals in bulk. For example, say you'll be eating 3oz of chicken for lunch for the next five days. Cook up a large batch of chicken and then measure out 3oz into five separate containers. Then do the same for a vegetable of your choice and a starch.

I can hear the groans right now, rejecting the thought of eating chicken every day, and believe me, I get it. Like the workouts I explained earlier, I want you to eat something you enjoy, but that is still a healthy choice.

It's usually easier to cook one protein source in batches, but you make the meal prep your own to stick with it. Alternate the protein and vegetable sources to keep from getting bored and falling back into unhealthy patterns.

How to Avoid Nutritional Sabotage

Unless you're one of the lucky few who are full-time authors, many of us will have a regular job to supplement our income. That's where nutritional traps can spring up, so I want you to be prepared.

In every office I've ever worked at, there has always been the temptation of starchy snacks lurking in every corner. It starts with bagels for a Monday meeting, then Friday donuts or pizza comes into play.

And it's always somebody's birthday, so cake and soda is a regular snack trap in the break room.

It's hard when meals are catered for an office event, and there's nothing available except the foods that are highest in sugar and fat. Offices turn to bagels, donuts, and pizza because...

1. They are easy to buy in bulk
2. They assume everyone likes those types of treats

As I mentioned, the best way to counter these landmines of nutritional sabotage is to pre-pack your lunches and healthy snacks. This way, when the pizza party starts, you can simply say: "No thank you," and indulge in your healthier option.

There's no need to feel guilty about it, either. Don't let your colleagues convince you to have one slice or donut. Inevitably, "just one" turns into several. Stick to your guns. You're on the road to a healthier lifestyle.

Nothing tastes as good as healthy feels.

You don't have to be anti-social either. There's no reason you can't join the birthday party or event, but being prepared with your own food will help you navigate those days when the temptation of sugary snacks is abundant.

You might even start a trend in your office and lead by example to the point where your co-workers will join you in your healthy journey. Then, the next time a party rolls around, more nutritional options may become available.

If these types of foods are in your own home, that's a different story and an easy fix. Throw them out! Replace those sugary snacks with some of the items I mentioned before. You'll be less tempted to reach for the bad foods when they aren't in your home.

7. Healthy Life Hacks

I've broken down the staples of wellness in the workplace, such as nutritional lunches, counteracting the effects of sitting, and getting in short bursts of exercise. But there are more small actions you can take to offset the daily grind and its impact on your health.

WHERE YOU PARK MATTERS

Fitness trackers have become trendy in the past few years. They measure your steps, heart rate, and many other variables that will keep your fitness on track for the day.

Want to increase those steps? Next time, park a little farther away from your office or when you go to the grocery store. It might not seem like much, but don't take for granted the ability to walk and use it as much as possible.

So, while achieving that perfect parking spot right by the door might be nice, know that movement is more important than status. Walking burns calories, increases blood flow, and lubricates the joints.

Get your steps in whenever you can!

USE IT OR LOSE IT: PRETENDING THE ELEVATOR IS BROKEN

I've had two trainers in my athletic career who both blew out their ACL. That's a muscle in your knee that keeps it stable. So, when it's ruptured, everyday movements are more challenging to complete.

I always keep this in mind when choosing between stairs, elevators, or even escalators. My choice will always be the stairs because the old adage "use it or lose it" is my first thought.

Your muscles will stay activated the more you choose options like using the stairs or parking further away. It also engages your cardiovascular health.

Ever climb a flight of stairs and feel winded after you get to the landing? I have, and whenever that happens, I know I need to work on my cardiovascular endurance more because that shouldn't be happening.

If you're struggling to catch your breath just by walking up the stairs, it's a direct sign from your body to make a change. If you suffer from asthma or another lung disorder, that's another matter, and you should follow your doctor's advice. But if you're a healthy adult, you have no excuse.

Start taking the stairs. Don't just stand on the escalator. Get your steps in and take control of your life! Taking the easier route may seem more convenient, but nothing worthwhile was ever easy.

If you work from home, start incorporating the other hack I told you about with the 30/60 rule. Set a timer, and for every 30 minutes of sitting, get up and perform 60 seconds of activity. Even if you're just walking around your living room, at least you're moving.

These small changes have a big effect and your body will thank you for it!

Why You Should Have Face-to-Face Meetings

Let's step back into an office for a minute for another healthy hack tip. Modern-day conveniences have extended how we communicate with each other. Text messages, email, and apps like Teams or Skype cause us to stay in our seats to converse with our colleagues.

If you work remotely, these tools are a great advancement and necessary to the success of your business. But if you work in an office environment and you're constantly sending messages or emails to co-workers, it's cementing you deeper in that chair.

Try something different. Next time you have a question for a co-worker, get up, walk over to their work area, and speak to them face-to-face. Not only does it keep you from remaining stagnant in your seat, but it's also a different dynamic when you have verbal communication instead of sending something through text and email.

We've become so preconditioned to technology that some of us have lost basic communication skills. Not only that, but it's very easy to read into a line of text or an email and put an inference into the tone the sender didn't have when writing it. How we absorb information has more to do with us and how we perceive the situation than what the sender intended. That stirs up all sorts of unnecessary drama.

When you get up and have a verbal conversation, it builds camaraderie and keeps a healthy working environment on a physical, mental, and emotional level. You never know; you could find a new office buddy just by conversing face-to-face.

Act Out Your Action Scenes

There are healthy hacks you can incorporate when working on your novel, too. For instance, writing an action scene can become more interactive. By that, I mean engaging your body alongside your mind to come up with compelling action scenes.

I used to teach a workshop that focused on movement to help authors depict more realistic fight scenes. Of course, I called it Fight Club, but unlike the rules in the novel, I'm going to talk about what we learned. The workshop aimed to get writers on their feet and have them learn about movement.

With my background in martial arts, I also had them strike focus mitts to feel what impact is like. It helped to draw up more sensory details. So, while you shouldn't get up and hit someone to act out your fight scenes, you can go through the motions.

Doing this will help write the scene AND get you up and moving. It's a win-win, and it can also be pretty fun. Just be careful! I had some students get a little carried away throwing their first punch. Back down to half speed, and you'll be well on your way to graduating from the Fight Club.

Developing Healthy Habits for Life

Office workers, especially those of us in the writing game, are at a higher risk for health issues because we spend so much time sitting at our desks. This guide is all about the urgent need for us to rethink our daily routines and start putting our health first.

These days, many authors find themselves glued to their chairs for eight hours or more each day. This kind of inactivity can lead to serious health problems. When you throw in unhealthy eating habits, the dangers of a sedentary lifestyle only get worse.

The truth is, the choices we make about what we eat and how much we move can seriously impact our health and how long we live.

However, there is hope! You can significantly improve your health outlook by swapping out unhealthy meals for nutritious ones and incorporating physical activity into your daily routine.

Simple changes, such as opting for whole foods rich in vitamins and minerals, can give your body the essential nutrients it needs to function optimally. Additionally, integrating regular exercise into your work day can counteract the negative effects of prolonged sitting.

A healthier lifestyle is built on making positive choices. The way you care for your body today will influence your health in the future. It's not just about avoiding unhealthy habits; it's about actively engaging in behaviors that promote well-being. This proactive approach can lead to increased energy levels, improved mood, and a greater sense of satisfaction in life.

To live a long and vibrant life, it's essential to adopt lifestyle habits that include a balanced diet, consistent exercise, and maintaining a healthy weight. This means not only focusing on what you eat but also being mindful of how much you move throughout the day.

Setting realistic goals, such as aiming for at least 150 minutes of moderate aerobic activity each week, can help you stay on track. Additionally, incorporating strength training exercises at least twice a week can enhance muscle mass and boost metabolism.

Moreover, it's important to recognize that lifestyle changes don't have to be overwhelming. Small, incremental adjustments can lead to significant improvements over time.

Just get started and see how feeling your best fuels your creativity!

STAYING FIT WHILE YOU SIT

Sneak Peek....

Writing Warrior

An Active Author Guide to
Overcoming Adversity and Achieving Goals

©2025 Cynthia Vespia

WARRIOR MENTALITY

What is warrior mentality?

Saying someone is a warrior can have many different meanings. Coming from the world of writing fiction, we may think of sword-wielding warriors going into battle. Those who spend time in the military might think of their brothers and sisters in arms as warriors. Someone battling a disease can also be referred to as a warrior.

So, when I talk about developing a "warrior mentality," it simply means a change in mindset to develop action that can conquer any challenge.

Warriors are those who face adversity head-on. But it's not so much about bravery leading them. They feel the fear but do it anyway because they know that's how you grow.

STAYING FIT WHILE YOU SIT

Remember this: We always regret the things we didn't do rather than the things we may have missed the mark on.

Because even if we tried and failed at something, at least we have that experience to draw from. So, when we make another attempt, we've already pierced the veil of uncertainty. We have a better idea of what we're up against and thus can create a mindset and action plan to obtain the goal next time.

We develop this mindset because the mind has power and influence over the rest of the body. Humans are remarkable in their abilities, but we cut off possibility by doubting ourselves. Strengthening your mentality can lead you to extraordinary heights.

I'll give you an example: Roger Bannister, born in Harrow, England, was a top mile-runner while studying at the University of Oxford in London. In 1954, Bannister did the unimaginable when he broke track and field's most notorious barrier: the four-minute mile.

Up to that point, many athletes tried and failed to run a mile in less than four minutes. After so many attempts were made, it was deemed an impossible feat. Then Bannister came along and shattered the previous record. His accomplishment also shattered the long-standing psychological mystique surrounding that feat.

After Bannister showed everyone it could be done, athletes started making even more triumphant records. It all comes back to mindset. Henry Ford once said, "Whether you think you can or you think you can't, you're right." Once Bannister proved breaking the four-minute mile could be done, it was no longer an insurmountable task.

When I first started competing in fitness events, I was nervous about it, but I dove right in to try. My first two years weren't great performances. Initially, I didn't know what I was up against. It was more of a feeling-out process that first year, and I actually wound up getting injured. That didn't stop me from returning the following year. However, my training was still off and it showed.

I remember having a conversation a short time later with jump rope educator and pioneer Buddy Lee about my lackluster performance. When I told him of my disappointment, he asked if I'd done everything I could do. Had I tried my very best? When I said yes, Buddy left me with the empowering words, "Then that's all you can do."

He said that putting in your best effort was nothing to feel ashamed of. When a US Olympic wrestler and 2X US Marine Best Athlete tells you something like that, you listen. So, I'm relating Buddy Lee's words of wisdom to you now to hit home my point.

By the time the third year of competition came around, I was dialed in. I made a plan for training and diet, stuck with it, and put up my best marks on several events. Through trial and error, I developed my warrior mentality to take on what initially seemed daunting. That focus and dedication allowed me to become the person I needed to be to conquer my personal challenge.

How do you become that person for yourself? Keep reading...

Dig Your Own Grave: Bury Your Past Self and Start a New Life

Have you ever looked at motivators like Tony Robbins or David Goggins and wondered where they got their discipline to build the lives they have now? Listening to them tell their own stories, I discovered an interesting fact. Both men created alter egos or 'alternative selves' that matched the life they envisioned having.

David Goggins became 'Goggins,' going from a broke, overweight bug exterminator to an athletic Navy SEAL who has broken multiple records. His mindset switched to a warrior mentality, which is now all about self-discipline. Becoming 'Goggins' allowed him to accomplish tasks that David maybe wouldn't have even attempted. Now, he's a best-selling author and motivator, and he recently became a smoke jumper fighting fires.

Tony Robbins talks a lot about how he "created this Tony Robbins guy." He's gone on in his teachings to explain how that shift in focus can work for anyone else being held back by past beliefs.

It's a method of writing down your goals and deciphering what type of person you need to become to achieve them. An example would be listing what you seek in a romantic partner and then asking yourself who you need to become to attract that type of person.

Don't get me wrong, it's not about closing away that past part of yourself in shame. It's more about growth and recognizing how certain patterns no longer serve you.

Put it another way: you're creating an alter ego who can do what needs to be done without faltering. Consider it your superhero side. Once the call comes out, you don your cape and get the job done with confidence. Athletes do this as well. It's a mental switch that primes the mind and body for accomplishing greatness.

Before stepping through the curtain for a fight, former UFC women's bantamweight champion and pro wrestling superstar Ronda Rousey embraces the pressure. She stated that the feeling of nervousness encouraged her.

> ***"This is what happens to my body before it does great things."*** **- Ronda Rousey (WWE 24 - Revolutionary: The Year of Ronda Rousey)**

Believe it or not, even Rousey was tapping into a different side of herself when stepping into the cage to fight or later when she became a pro wrestler. She is the epitome of focusing on a goal and putting together a long-term plan for attaining it.

Where David Goggins may not have seen himself reaching his full potential, his alternative self 'Goggins' gives him a different mindset—a warrior mentality.

Having this alter ego is simply a way of empowering yourself to break the barriers that are holding you back from your true potential. It doesn't mean you're splitting up your personality, rather, you're permitting your alternative self to access traits you may otherwise shy away from.

These traits can be anything from courage, confidence, or even embracing levity during a challenging time. Whatever you need to access in the moment, your warrior self is your drive to do it readily without second-guessing everything.

Professional wrestlers and actors are well known (and well paid) for accessing an alternative self. To perform at top levels, they must tap into emotions they don't usually carry in their everyday lives.

The 14-time women's wrestling champion Ashley Fliehr, aka WWE Superstar Charlotte Flair, has said at times she wished Ashley had some of the traits that 'Charlotte' possesses.

To become Charlotte Flair and perform in front of the largest live crowds around the world, Ashley switches gears and shifts into the persona of Charlotte: a brash, cagey, confident woman who carries herself like a goddess and backs it up with exceptional athleticism.

Most professional wrestlers will tell you that their characters are just extensions of themselves with the volume turned way up. There's no reason you can't do the same thing. We just have to tap into that mindset first. The one that empowers you in your pursuits rather than deters you.

Would it surprise you if I said you already access different parts of your personality in different situations? Think about it. You're a certain way at work that differs from the way you are at home. You act differently with your friends than with your in-laws. And so on. But have you ever been that other side of yourself when you needed to be? Have you intentionally 'turned up the volume' in a way that empowers you and taps into your warrior mentality?

If not, the good news is we're going to discover your warrior spirit together. So, bury your past self and prepare to start a new life.

Learn More in Writing Warrior: An Active Author Guide to Overcoming Adversity and Achieving Goals

Available now!

Acknowledgments

I've had a great deal of influences in the world of fitness. First and foremost, my older brother Charlie was an amateur bodybuilding champion and martial artist. Like most young men, he gained his knowledge and passion for fitness from watching Arnold Schwarzenegger. I gained mine from watching my brother. We lost him in 1996 but his spirit and passion for fitness live on through me.

I have also been fortunate to have some great trainers along my journey as well. They've instructed me in the weight room, on the field, and through various martial arts disciplines like Brazilian Jiu-Jitsu; Muay Tai; Kali; Savate; and Jeet Kune Do. So, my many thanks go to Ray Inta, Blaze Khounsaname, Kelly Decolati, Jeannie Paparone, Tony Pearson, GrandMaster Rashim, Master Nick Blomgren, Diana Lee Inosanto, and Ron Balicki for their contributions to my learning.

I'm also not without my own inspirations, some of whom I've had the pleasure of meeting, and they continue to inspire me for their work ethic and the way they motivate others. So, a shout-out goes to 4-time IFBB Figure Olympia Champion Nicole Wilkins; Fitness Model Jamie Eason; Women's Physique

Champion Dana Linn Bailey; Celebrity Trainer Ashley Conrad; Dr. Jim Stoppani; Fitness Stars Ashley Horner and Hannah Eden, Fitness Trainer Kris Gethin, and Fitness Model and Motivational Speaker Greg Plitt.

Greg unfortunately passed away in 2015. He left behind a legacy not just of fitness but of inspiration. I hope that somehow within these pages you find a little bit of inspiration to keep you going through your day.

Live your dreams. -Cyn

READ ALL THE ACTIVE AUTHOR GUIDES

- Staying Fit as You Sit: Active Author Guide for Wellness in the Workplace

- Writing Warrior: An Active Author Guide to Overcoming Adversity and Achieving Goals

- Keeping Your Fiction in Shape: Active Author Guide for Building the Body of a Book

- Changing the Dialogue: Active Author Guide to Calm the Mind and Reboot the Creative Process

- Plotting the Course: Active Author Guide to Increase Productivity and End Procrastination

- Creating the Character: Active Author Guide to Building a Memorable Brand

Get easy, actionable tips for whole body health right to your inbox with the newsletter. Sign up and receive the Healthy Habits Toolkit to help get you started! www.cynthiavespia.com/writerwellness

ABOUT THE AUTHOR

I'm a former competitive athlete, certified trainer, fantasy author and fitness writer. I have over 12 years of experience as a life coach in physical training and motivation.

My novels are a gritty mix of fantasy, magic, and the supernatural while exploring the theme of "success through struggle." I've also written content for Microsoft, UFC, WWE, HBO, Netflix, and more.

By combining my love of writing and wellness, it's my aim to educate and motivate fellow authors and busy creative professionals to a healthier version of themselves.

Because feeling your best fuels creativity!

STAY UP-TO-DATE

Official Site:
www.cynthiavespia.com/writerwellness

Instagram: @originalcynwrites
Facebook:
https://www.facebook.com/originalcynwrites
Youtube:
https://www.youtube.com/c/OriginalCynWrites

NOVELS BY CYNTHIA VESPIA

A TIME OF DRAGONS
(adventure fantasy)
Rayna the Dragonslayer
Rayna the Dragon Warrior
Rayna the Dragon Rider

SILKES STRIKE FORCE
(superhero urban fantasy)
Karma
Kobra
Kaged
Khaos

VEGAS VIGILANTES
(dark urban fantasy)
Casino Empire
Lucky Sevens
Vegas Valkyries
Sin City Assassin

DEMON HUNTERS
(heroic adventure fantasy)
Demon Hunter Saga
Demon Huntress Legends

OTHER BOOKS
The Crescent
Theater of Pain
Sins and Virtues
Be Your Own Superhero

References

1. Mayo Foundation for Medical Education and Research. Sitting is the new smoking " mayo clinic connect. Mayo Clinic. https://connect.mayoclinic.org/blog/living-with-mild-cognitive-impairment-mci/newsfeed-post/sitting-is-the-new-smoking/
2. Why everyone keeps saying "sitting is the new smoking" - tri-city medical center. Tri. (2018, December 29). https://www.tricitymed.org/2017/07/everyone-keeps-saying-sitting-new-smoking/
3. Large amounts of sedentary time linked to higher risk of dementia in older adults. University of Arizona News. (2023, September 13). https://news.arizona.edu/story/large-amounts-sedentary-time-linked-higher-risk-dementia-older-adults
4. Study Links Time Spent Sitting to Higher Risk of Death from 14 Diseases. American Cancer Society. https://pressroom.cancer.org/PatelSedentary2018
5. Standing Up for Your Health. Doctors of Osteopathic Medicine. https://findado.osteopathic.org/standing-health
6. Billy GG, Lemieux SK, Chow MX. Lumbar disc changes associated with prolonged sitting. PM R. 2014;6(9):790-5. doi:10.1016/j.pmrj.2014.02.014

7. American Academy of Orthopedic Surgeons. OrthoInfo. Cervical radiculopathy.
8. Park JH, Moon JH, Kim HJ, Kong MH, Oh YH. Sedentary lifestyle: overview of updated evidence of potential health risks. Korean J Fam Med. 2020;41(6):365-373. doi:10.4082/kjfm.20.0165
9. Baker R, Coenen P, Howie E, Williamson A, Straker L. The short term musculoskeletal and cognitive effects of prolonged sitting during office computer work. Int J Environ Res Public Health. 2018;15(8):1678. doi:10.3390/ijerph15081678
10. (n.d.). Dowager's Hump: What It Is, Diagnosis, and Treatment Options. Clear Scoliosis Institute. https://clear-institute.org/blog/dowagers-hump/
11. Computer Vision Syndrome. Cleveland Clinic. https://my.clevelandclinic.org/health/diseases/24802-computer-vision-syndrome
12. Static and dynamic postural loadings during computer work in females: Sitting on an office chair versus sitting on an exercise ball. ScienceDirect. https://www.sciencedirect.com/science/article/abs/pii/S0003687008000690
13. Sitting on a gym ball at work – The facts. PosturePeople. https://posturepeople.co.uk/sitting-gym-ball-work-facts/
14. Standing Desks: How They Help You Beat Inactivity. WebMD. https://www.webmd.com/fitness-exercise/standing-desks-help-beat-inactivity#1-2

15. Honeycutt, H. (2023, May 26). How to Choose the Best Standing Desk. Lowes. https://www.lowes.com/n/buying-guide/standing-desk-buying-guide
16. Repetitive Motion Injuries. ColumbiaDoctors. https://www.columbiadoctors.org/specialties/rehabilitation-regenerative-medicine/conditions/repetitive-motion-injuries
17. Stoppani, J., PhD (2024, November 15). Sitting is the New Smoking. Jim Stoppani. https://www.jimstoppani.com/health/sitting-is-the-new-smoking
18. (2022, March 22). Benefits of massage therapy. Mayo Clinic. https://www.mayoclinichealthsystem.org/hometown-health/speaking-of-health/benefits-of-massage-therapy
19. (2022, March 27). David Goggins on Stretching and Releasing a Tight Psoas Muscle. Mobility Athlete. https://mobilityathlete.com/david-goggins-psoas-stretching/
20. How much physical activity do you need? American Heart Association. https://www.heart.org/en/healthy-living/fitness/fitness-basics/aha-recs-for-physical-activity-infographic
21. American Heart Association Recommendations for Physical Activity in Adults and Kids | American Heart Association
22. What Are the Benefits of Aerobic Exercise? Healthline. https://www.healthline.com/health/fitness-

exercise/benefits-of-aerobic-exercise#benefits

23. 14 Benefits of Strength Training. Healthline. https://www.healthline.com/health/fitness/benefits-of-strength-training#benefits
24. (n.d.). Why Being Flexible Is Great for Your Health. Healthline. https://www.healthline.com/health/benefits-of-flexibility
25. Ross A, Friedmann E, Bevans M, Thomas S. National survey of yoga practitioners: Mental and physical health benefits. Complement Ther Med. 2013;21(4):313-23. doi:10.1016/j.ctim.2013.04.001
26. Ikai S, Uchida H, Mizuno Y, et al. Effects of chair yoga therapy on physical fitness in patients with psychiatric disorders: A 12-week single-blind randomized controlled trial. J Psychiatr Res. 2017;94:194-201. doi:10.1016/j.jpsychires.2017.07.015
27. Why Eating Breakfast is so Important. Reframe Nutrition. https://www.reframenutrition.org/post/why-is-eating-breakfast-so-important
28. 5 Things That Happen to Your Body When You Skip Meals. Banner Health. https://www.bannerhealth.com/healthcareblog/teach-me/here-is-what-happens-when-you-skip-meals
29. Pedre, V. M., M.D. (5/16/22). What Is A Caffeine Crash? Plus, 4 MD Tips To Prevent It From Happening. Mind Body Green. https://www.mindbodygreen.com/articles/caffeine-crash

30. Seol JE, Cho GJ, Jang SH, Ahn SW, Hong SM, Park SH, Kim H. Effect of Amount of Daily Water Intake and Use of Moisturizer on Skin Barrier Function in Healthy Female Participants. Ann Dermatol. 2024 Jun;36(3):145-150. doi: 10.5021/ad.23.067. PMID: 38816975; PMCID: PMC11148315.
31. Water: How much should you drink every day? Mayo Clinic. https://www.mayoclinic.org/healthy-lifestyle/nutrition-and-healthy-eating/in-depth/water/art-200442

www.ingramcontent.com/pod-product-compliance
Lightning Source LLC
Chambersburg PA
CBHW071901070526
44583CB00016B/1794